A Tiny Book on Energy Work

A tiny book on energy work

by Kellie Fitzgerald

Nothing in this book is to be taken as medical advice or medical treatments.

Table of Contents

Forward

When I first set out to write this book I wanted it to be small because so many beginners get overwhelmed when facing the sheer amount of information on this topic.   I also wanted it to give you the basics, enough of a foundation for those who want to go deeper into energy work, yet also just enough to give those wanting basic explanations of how things work. Hopefully I have accomplished all of that and perhaps a bit more.

You might be wondering exactly who I am to write this book in the first place. Well, I've studied energy work and much more for a very, very long time. I've studied with masters and with those who were more of a contemporary nature. Perhaps guiding others along their spiritual journey is where I've learned the most. One glance at my personal library will reveal I have collected dozens and dozens of books on topics such as Reiki, martial arts, esoteric energy methods and much more in addition to the rest of my metaphysical library.   Basically I'm a teacher, truthseeker an intuitive and a healer. I wrote this book because I believe with all my heart you are those things as well.

Please feel free to reach out if you come across something in this book you want to dive deeper into. I do give individual classes all the time on a variety of things and I'd love the opportunity to work with you.

Introduction

So what exactly is "energy work?" Well, the short answer is that energy work helps rebalance the body's energy system so that it flows through the body rather than getting stuck somewhere. If you've ever had stuck energy you've probably experienced it as a feeling of just not feeling "well." Stuck energy can have an impact on everything from our joints to our emotions to how we think. Brain fog anyone?   In my experience that is usually due to stuck energy.

There are many modalities for performing energy work ranging from acupuncture and Reiki to EFT (Emotional Freedom Technique), breathwork, Pranic and Quantum healing, massage, working with crystals, working with affirmations and so many more. This book is not designed to do anything but offer a foundation to understanding what energy work and energy healing really are (I am not a doctor so do not interpret anything within this book as medical advice).

Understand you can study whatever modality you want, you can pick one or many. What it comes down to though is that you must ultimately practice whichever one resonates with you. This is not a one-size-fits-all world and that goes for energy work too. While I do find value in studying as many as you can find I also know that you will come to find one or two that speak to your heart and soul. Those are the ones to do the deep dive with. Oh and yes you can take concepts and practices from several and

combine them into your very own type of energy
work too! Just wait until you've studied for a while
first.

First things first

Everything is energy. Yes, it's true. I know, to many minds it just doesn't make sense but science has indeed proven everything is energy. If you'd like additional information on how this works please do yourself a favor and find a book you resonate with about the subject, there are many excellent ones available. Quantum physics is an excellent thing to study and really isn't as difficult to understand as many people believe.

Once you accept that everything truly is energy it only makes sense to accept that we are all connected, that what we think about we really do draw into our lives and that if we're really having a difficult time in life we might be drawing those difficulties into our lives. No judgement. Just notice what you think about most.

Einstein said "Everything is energy. Match the frequency of the reality you want and you cannot help but get that reality. It can be no other way. This is not philosophy. This is physics."

So exactly how does this work? Well from an energetic standpoint whatever you focus on is what you draw into your reality. Have you ever played the game where you focus on a particular color or type of car and realized you see them everywhere? That's a simple way of showing how powerful our thoughts really are. Yet, many people just can't believe they are creating their own realities.

It is difficult to understand how someone could create trauma or illness in their life, yet that is exactly what scientists have shown is happening. Your perception of your reality is as important, if not more so, than what is actually happening in your life. In most cases we have to let go of what we've been told in order to see what is actually true. For example if you've always been told money is the root of evil then you are likely to have financial difficulties in your adult life, whereas someone else who was told money is only a tool to be used in life will likely have an easier time financially.

No one has ever said it is an easy thing to do to let go of the programming you've received throughout your life, however, if you want things to change you absolutely must deprogram yourself.   Learn to utilize your life energy to help you through that process.

One tool I've often given to my students is a short meditation involving what is known as the violet flame. Though the manner in which I have my students utilize it is as a beautiful purple rain shaft gently washing over them. If you visualize this purple shower washing over your entire body while washing away any negativity, illness or stress to be transmuted into mother earth it will help you change your way of thinking. Persistence is key here, don't expect things to shift immediately. You will have to work at it. For some people changes happen quicker than others. Again, no judgement, just pay attention to your thoughts as you go through this process. And it is a process.

What Do You Mean Raise My Vibration?

That you should raise your vibration is said so much these days I'm pretty sure even the masters are beginning to wonder what it means. If as I've written, everything is energy, it stands to reason that everything has it's own vibration. The simple statement is to bring something you want into your life you have to adjust your vibration to match it. Easy enough right? Well, no, not really.

There are many different ways people have used to raise their vibration. By far the most effective in my opinion is to practice gratitude. I tell my students to start a gratitude journal and find something to add to it every day. Understand it does take some time to feel this working but it does work. Look around you right now and find three things you are grateful for. Most likely these won't be huge things, but they certainly can be. One of my students recently closed on their house. Definitely a huge thing to be grateful for. But they can also be grateful for the flowers blooming in their new yard, the cool breeze coming through the trees and the experience of moving into their new home.

Find something to be grateful for every day and you will definitely raise your vibration.

Meditation is another way to raise your vibration. I know, I know, I heard the groan. Hear me out though, meditation doesn't have to be difficult. If you are one of those people, like myself, who has trouble sitting still for a period of time you can always do a moving meditation. Take a slow walk in nature. Look around as you walk. Feel the air temperature, hear the sounds around you, really be present while you are outside. Staying present, to me, is also a type of meditation. Just be. I know we're taught we should stay busy, but I find the people who really detest meditation are also those people who are never really in the present moment.

One easy exercise I give people who are not fond of either sitting still or being quiet and present is to simply practice doing nothing. Not a thing. No tv or music, no computer or phone, nothing. Just sit or stand and do nothing. Feel your breath entering and leaving your body. Listen to the silence, or lack thereof. Don't look around and see all the things you should be doing, they can wait for a few minutes. Just sit with yourself. Notice what you think and how you feel. If the thought that you're being lazy comes up, and it probably will, just dismiss it. Notice and dismiss every other thought.

Do this at least once a day for a week. You can start with just one single minute if you want. Work up to at least ten minutes. Guess what? That's meditation. One of the best ways to raise your vibration.

Another great way of raising your vibration is forgiveness. If you've never made a practice of forgiveness it's way past time that you did. I encourage people to write letters of forgiveness to anyone they feel did them wrong. Do not mail or otherwise deliver the letters. These letters are for you to get the drama or trauma out of your system. You can write as nicely or as unkindly as you want. You're not going to let anyone else see them. Just make sure to end your letter with "I forgive you and me and the whole situation."   The reason I have people do this exercise is because we store drama, pain, trauma and all those other wounds inside our bodies. Writing letters addressing the situation and having our say begins to remove the damage from our bodies and really our souls too. If you feel this is a silly thing to do then make your letter silly, if you're writing and tears come let them fall. Just get it out of your body and forgive it. It might take several tries but I promise you it's well worth the effort.   Then forgive yourself for allowing those damaging things to happen to you and for holding on to them for so long. Let them go. All of it. If it helps you to rip up your letters or burn them (safely please) or bury them or throw pieces into the ocean...do it. Do whatever it takes to get you to the point where you can be in forgiveness.

Love is a powerful way to raise your vibration and it's one I feel people do not use enough. People often have a misconstrued conception of what love really is. Love is really everything. Love doesn't have anything really to do with sex or being in a relationship. Love simply is. Think about someone you love, either currently or in the past. What comes to mind? Probably something about how kind they were or what a wonderful guy/girl they were. Think about a time where you loved your job or car or motorcycle or pet. You probably have similar feeling about those things. They were wonderful, they were fun or whatever. Allow yourself to feel love.

Once you've focused on feeling love for someone or something that has been in your life look around you and find out what else you love. Maybe it's something that was a gift from a deceased loved one. Maybe it's a pet or a tree or a flower or whatever. Practice feeling love for everything in general. When you can get to the point where you can feel love just by thinking about love you've raised your vibration enough to create wonderful things in your life. Remember that love truly is always the answer.

While there are many other ways of raising your vibration I do find gratitude and love to be the quickest and most lasting ways to do so. One other that I'd like to include here is positive thinking. I'm certain you've encountered positive affirmations somewhere along the way. While those certainly are part of positive thinking there's more to it than that.

If you have a picnic planned and it starts to rain that morning how do you feel? Do you immediately curse the rain and declare the day ruined? Do you decide to just move your picnic inside and still have a great time? Postive thinking means that you change your perception of what's going "wrong" so that you can see how things are actually going "right." Of course sometimes things happen that are just horrible things and changing your perception is not only incredibly difficult for painful. In those instances you can still find something to be positive about, even if it's a tiny little thing.

Naturally positive people tend to be healthier and happier than those who haven't quite figured out how to incorporate positivity into their lives. You might know people who are always positive and you have probably wondered how things always seem to go right for them. They aren't positive because things have gone right, things have gone right because they're positive. Like most of what is contained within this book being positive is a choice. I'm not going to tell you that you have to become positive in order to have great things in your life. That is your choice. But I can tell you from experience in my own life that I've dug myself out of some pretty dark places after making the decision to be more positive. Like everything else it's a process.

Now that you've learned everything is energy and has a vibration and a few ways to raise your vibration let's go a bit deeper into energy work. The truth of it is you can be meditating, forgiving, loving and thinking positive thoughts and still things just don't seem to be moving forward for you. Sometimes there is an issue you don't know anything about, perhaps your chakras aren't balanced or one is blocked.

What are Chakras Anyway?

I decided to talk about chakras simply because they are so vitally important to everything else in this book. Making certain your chakras are balanced properly really is the key to beginning your spiritual journey and learning about energy work. The simplest way to look at chakras is to understand they are energy points in our bodies. It is not within the scope of this book to do a deep dive into the chakra system but I will give you the basics. Visualize each chakra as a spinning sphere.

Beginning at the base of your spine is the root chakra, it is red in color. This chakra is your foundation energetically. If you are feeling ungrounded, like you have no sense of support or terribly unsettled it is likely your root chakra is not balanced. You can help yourself by visualizing a red spinning sphere getting bigger and brighter at the base of your spine. Of course there are many other methods, but I find most people want something quick and easy and this will do the trick.

Moving up from the base of your spine to roughly between your pelvis and your navel is your sacral chakra. The sacral chakra is orange in color. This is referred to as the second chakra and is the place where our emotions, sexual energy and creativity are housed in the body. Many believe kidney and urinary tract health are also located in this place. If you are feeling completely out of control emotionally, are unable to do creative things that usually come naturally to you or are having issues relating to sexual health it is likely your sacral chakra is out of balance. Just as with the root chakra you can help yourself by visualizing an orange sphere in the location of your sacral chakra. You can also eat orange fruits and vegetables or wear orange. Your intention is always key so make sure you do set the intention to balance your chakras while you are working with each of them individually.

About three inches above your navel and pretty close to the center of your body is your solar plexus chakra. This is what I refer to as your personal power chakra and it is yellow in color. Use the techniques above to assist in balancing this chakra, making sure to use the color yellow, as you do so. If you are lacking self-esteem, confidence or are generally feeling powerless in any situation you are probably suffering from a blocked or out of balance solar plexus. With this chakra I like to have people do the previously-mentioned techniques but also to go outside and "soak up the sun" for a while. When this chakra is balanced you feel "sunny" in disposition and are ready to tackle anything that comes across your path, usually with a smile.

Your heart chakra is, as expected, located in the center of your chest and is green in color. You might have heard that some people have a pink heart chakra color and that is correct, you just don't need to focus on that right now. If you are feeling like you've lost your connection to others, if you feel depression, anxious, lonely and just generally like you don't belong anywhere...chances are very high that you have a blocked or out of balance heart chakra. You can always do the same techniques I've already given you, substituting green for the other colors. I've found however that these days our heart chakras need just a little bit more care though. Walking in nature and noticing all the green around you is a wonderful way to unblock your heart. Wear green, eat greens, visualize a beautiful green color coming out of your heart and surrounding your body with a big, green hug. Be kind to yourself. You have to love yourself first before anyone else truly can. Set the intention to open your heart every day until you're feeling better about things.

Moving up to the base of your throat is your throat chakra, it is blue in color. There can be variations in the hue of blue from person to person but most often it is a light sky blue color. This chakra governs how you communicate and how you show up for the world. If you've been abused previously this chakra will almost always be blocked. Even if you've never experienced abuse this chakra can be blocked. If you're very shy, don't communicate well, have thyroid issues, frequent sore throats and even infections in your throat or mouth...your throat chakra needs some attention. Please do use techniques given above and set the attention to communicate clear and effectively. Set intentions to heal any and all infections and issues. Note that medically diagnosed thyroid issues still need medical treatment and these techniques are not a substitute for that. However it's been shown repeatedly that energy work can benefit medical treatment.

Your third eye chakra is a beauiful indigo/purple color and is located in the cente of your forehead. Of all the chakras people seem to be interested most in this one. This is the seat of our intuition and spirituality. While it might be tempting to begin with working on this one, you really do need to establish a healthy foundation with healthy and balanced first through fifth chakras first. The third eye chakra regulates the pituitary gland. Trying to work first with your third eye can produce feeling of floating, flakiness and generally unwellness. I urge you to, at least initially, work with chakras in order. Having said that there are some things you can do to balance this chakra. Begin with previous techniques, they really do work. In addition you may find yoga and meditation to be essential to opening your third eye if that is your quest. Do not try to rush this one, it simply will not work. This is a process. If you want to strengthen your intuition, and that is why most people want to work with their third eye chakra, you have to take your time. Don't take this lightly.

At the top of your head is your crown chakra. Most often this is a violet type color but it can also be a brilliant silvery while. This chakra connects you to the "all" of the universe, the divine, God or whatever name you use. This is the seat of expanded consciousness and if your crown chakra is balanced you will experience inner peace and a profound sense of purpose and belonging to everything. It is believed this is the most powerful of the seven chakras and if it is unbalanced you can experience headaches, a lack of empathy, confusion and other symptoms. If you come to believe your crown chakra is unbalanced begin with the previously-given techniques. This is a good time to start finding crystals that resonate with you. Holding a clear quartz or amethyst while you meditate is a wonderful method of unblocking the crown chakra. There are many yoga poses the will assist with this as well. Listen to yourself, your own inner knowing, and give yourself permission to play around with various techniques until you find the one or ones that resonate with you.

There are other chakras and many other methods of unblocking them but I hope you've gotten at least a little bit of knowledge so you can help yourself explore and work with these seven chakras. Truly there is no right or wrong way to help yourself here. If you are a fan of crystals, match the color with the chakra and go with it. Incense? Same thing, match the scent with the chakra. Foods, clothing, sounds and meditations can all be tools for you to use along your journey. Play with it. Have fun.

Reiki

Since I am a Reiki Master/Teacher I have decided to begin this section of this book with talking about Reiki. Reiki is a type of alternative medicine or energy healing that originated in Japan. Reiki practitioners use a type of healing whereby divine universal enegy is channeled through the top of the practitioner's head down through their heart and out the palms of their hands. In most cases the practitioner doesn't even actually touch the person they are working on as energy flows where it is needed. This energy work promotes healing, stress relief, relaxation and pain relief among many others.

It is important here to note that Reiki does not replace traditional medical treatment but can support those treatments. While not specific on types of injury or disease Reiki is used for it has been shown to be extremely helpful in promoting calmness and peace in patients receiving treatment of all types. This creates a sort of support system for the traditional medical treatments to build on.

While not well known in the past, today Reiki practitioners often visit hospitals, medical offices and even nursing homes. I've even used Reiki on hospice patients as a form of stress-relief and pain reduction.

Though practitioners study for years to become proficient Reiki Masters and/or Teachers there are some simple ways you can use the energy of Reiki for yourself. Please note you will not be channeling actual Reiki but you will be using the same principals. It is also important to realize the energy Reiki practitioners channel and the energy you will be working with, does not come from either the practitioner or from you. This is energy from the universe, divine energy, God energy, whatever name you want to give it energy. By utilizing this energy from what I refer to as "source" the practitioner receives energy as well as their client. Definitely a bonus.

What do you do when you stub your toe or bump your elbow? You grab the injured body part, right? That is the basis of energy healing. We instinctively know there are nerve endings which are screaming for attention so we apply pressure. When you are working with energy healing you are just adding the energy flow to what you are already doing.

Hold your hands about six inches apart with your palms facing each other. Feel the warmth between them?   It's almost as if they are magnetically attracted to each other. That's energy flowing.   As an experiment here I want you to put one of your hands on one of your knees palm down. Now pay attention to how your knee feels. Is it warm or cool? Remember this sensation.

Now I want you to visualize a bright beam of white light coming down from the heavens and entering the top of your head. Feel this white light as it moves through your body all the way to your hands.

Feel the energy moving from your palm to your knee. Sense the difference?

Remembering the information on chakras now turn the light that enters the top of your head a color that matches your solar plexus chakra. That's yellow. Now place your hands on your solar plexus and visualize the now yellow light flowing from the palms of your hands into your solar plexus. What sensations do you feel? I refer to this process as "running energy" because that's what you're doing even if it takes you a little practice to feel it.

Repeat this with the rest of your chakras until you become familiar with how the different chakras feel and how the energy feels flowing from your palms. I began with the Solar Plexus simply because it is the body's center of energy and your power center. You will find it most helpful to begin at your Root Chakra and move up from there in order.

As a side note you might try this energetic method on loved ones and even on pets. Animals are especially sensative to energy and often really enjoy receiving energy from their owners. Also next time a loved one asks for a shoulder rub try running energy and see if they notice the difference. You might be amazed.

Some Other Modalities of Energy Work

EFT is an alternative treatment wherein you use your fingers to tap on the 12 meridian points in order to relieve pain, emotional distress or other "discomforts." In recent years EFT has become more popular and there are tons of books and information online that will give you precise information on this technique if you have an interest. I have found many people disregard this alternative treatment because it seems so simple to do. Please do not make this mistake. This is an incredibly powerful alternative treatment.

Acupuncture utilizes points along these same meridians to insert very small needles to remove energetic blocks and allow energy to flow throughout the body. Again there is much information readily available about this technique.

Massage therapy is of course one of the most widely-utilized alternative treatments and will definitely relieve pain and support healing throughout the body. You can find a good massage therapist just about anywhere these days. If you are truly concerned about energy blockages you would be well-advised to seek a massage therapist who works with Shiatsu as well as other types of massage. Often massage therapists work with chiropractors and combining chiropractic treatments with massage therapy is an amazing experience everyone should treat themselves to.

Chiropractors train for many years and pass many exams in order to treat patients. If you've never been to a chiropractor you've missed out on a terrific way to feel better and generally be on your way to better health. Chirpractors usually work with the musculosketal system and often advise specific stretches and exercises to their patients as well as manipulate the spine and often other joints in the body.

Reflexology is a type of massage that uses pressure on specific pressure points on your ears, hands and feet in order to promote and support pain relief and healing. While not as common as a more mainstream massage therapy this is a very useful tool to have in your life.

Craniosacral therapy uses gently hand movements with a light touch to investigate fluid movements around your central nervous system and from personal experience is very useful for the relief of migraine headaches as well as many other types of headaches, stress and even can help with your balance.

Everyone has heard of yoga in it's various types. Yoga is an excellent way to support general well-being and stress relief. You can find a type of yoga that will work for you no matter what shape you are in. Just remember to be gentle with yourself.

Like yoga there are martial arts that are wonderful methods of generating a feeling of peace and well-being. I'm sure you've probably seen a group of people in a park somewhere practicing Tai Chi. There are many other variations available.

Yes all of these alternative treatments can raise your vibration. This is a very limited list of energy treatments available. Of course there are many, many additional modalities and I encourage you to do your own investigation to find one or two that resonate with you. Remember to start simply with whatever modality you choose. Anything you do to balance and center yourself, relieve pain and stress or just generally feel better will raise your vibration.

What About Crystals?

Of course if everything is energy and has it's own vibration it would figure that crystals also have their own energetic vibrations.   There are countless crystals available on the market now and you are free to pick and choose the ones that resonate with you. I'm just giving you suggestions on which ones to begin with.   One of the most commonly asked questions I get from students is about what crystals to use for what purpose.   The real answer is whichever one calls to you.   I always recommend people begin with a clear quartz crystal though. Whatever shape or size you want. As you work with crystals you will find you are drawn to certain shapes but initially it really doesn't matter.

Being clear this crystal can be used for whatever you want to use it for.   Seriously.   Generally speaking clear quartz has a protective and restorative energy. It is often used to amplify the properties of other crystals and is the first stone I always recommend people get.   Many people use clear quartz in manifesting meditations but really you can use this one for just about anything.

Amethyst is available in a variety of purple hues and I've even seen what is referred to as pink amethyst recently. This is a very calming stone which is often used to bring clarity and peace in meditations. If you are drawn to this crystal you might just need more calm, peace and emotional balance in your life.

Rose Quartz is available in a wide variety of pink colors. This crystal is associated with love, friendship and deep inner healing. When a client has gone through a break-up or lost a loved one I recommend carrying a rose quartz in their pocket for a while. Many people use rose quartz for protection and to get rid of bad vibes. This is one of the most popular crystals.

Carnelian is an orange crystal sometimes more yellowish and sometimes more red. Carnelian is the stone of courage and positive life changes and choices. It is also used for support of the reproductive system in both men and women as well as to heal any sexual disfunction. Many people utilize carnelian to help with auto-immune issues as well as a variety of other issues.

Lapis Lazuli is a deep blue color and is used to work with spirit guides as well as to support the throat chakra. It is a very protective stone and is known to not only repel negative energy but can return it to it's source. Believed to releave anger and dark thoughts this is a great stone to keep around.

Black Obsidian is great to have to see the truth in situations as well as to stop the bad habits we develop that keep us from achieving our goals. Being a black crystal it is also protective and often used to absorb dark energy. If used for this purpose make sure to cleanse your crystal often.

Black Tourmaline is the stone most people use to absorb dark energy and is most often used to stagnant or blocked energy. Personally I use Black Obsidian and Black Tourmaline interchangeably depending on which stone I'm drawn to at the time.

Citrine can be light yellow to bright orange and is a terrific crystal for beginners to use because of it's ability to being prosperity and success during times of change and spiritual growth. It brings on positive energy and a deeper connection with your core being. Often people who have gone through a traumatic experience will meditate while holding a citrine due to the positive and spiritual nature of the stone.

Hematite is a silvery colored stone with a high iron content, because of the high iron this stone is often associated with supporting the blood. Hematite is widely considered the most powerful grounding stone and is used to convey confidence and to overcome vices.

This has been a very brief overview of many of the most commonly found crystals. If you feel compelled to do so please do your own research on these and other crystals. Remember to rely on your own inner guidance system when choosing crystals or any other spiritual tools as what resonates for you might not be what resonates with others.

Just a note about purchasing crystals. Make sure you look for reputable retailers both brick and mortar stores and online. There are a lot of places who sell fake crystals or dyed crystals. Make sure you know what you're buying.

There is also much to be said for picking up a rock you find outside that you are particularly attracted to. In many areas you can find different types of agates and quartz on the ground without much difficulty. These rocks can be used just as you would use a crystal. Feel the energy of the rock and decide what intention you want to set for using that particular rock. For example I have a piece of agate I found years ago that I use when I want to feel happy and peaceful. I know it sounds odd to feel the energy of a rock but if you allow yourself to practice a bit it will all begin to make sense.

Movement

Yes movement. Moving your body is one of the quickest ways to raise your vibration as it literally moves energy throughout your body. I've already mentioned yoga and going for a walk but there are as many ways to move as there are people moving.

Dance is a wonderful way to raise your vibration because it usually combines movement with music which is also known to increase energy flow. It doesn't matter if you're a good dancer or not and truthfully sometimes the worse you dance the more you laugh and that does a lot of raise your vibration itself.

Even just a little bit of exercise will also raise your vibration. Something as simple as stretching or going for a walk or run works wonders. With everything else in this book make sure you don't try to do too much too fast or you will injure yourself and undo all the good you've done.

Truly it doesn't matter how you move as long as you do. Not only is it a tremendous health benefit you'll be raising your vibration at the same time. You'll feel better too.

How Do You Manifest?

If you've read this far and done all the exercises described in this book you're in good shape to put all of this to work manifesting those things you want to bring into your life. As I mentioned towards the beginning of the book, if you've tried affirmations and they've not worked for you then you probably have energy blockages somewhere. Now that you've done some energy work to raise your vibration you will want to try those affirmations again.

People are always wanting a shortcut, they want the shortest route to where they're going, they want instant results when they're working for something and really most people just don't want to put the time and effort into manifesting what they want. If this sounds like you, first off, know you are not alone. However, you need to make the decision now to actually put in the work to manifest what you want. This is no instant gratification thing.

The first step I have people do is to really define and get absolutely clear on what it is they really want. Many people say "I want money." But is that really true? Sure everyone needs money to buy things and even just to live in today's world, but is it money that really makes you happy? When you go deeper into what it is you want you will probably find you want what money can buy or do for you, not just the money itself. If you're focusing on the wrong things you will manifest those things that really don't make you happy. Ask yourself questions about what you truly want until you are clear on what it is.

Once you've settled on exactly what you wish to manifest write it down. Write it down several places so you will see it multiple times every day. I know this sounds like putting affirmations everywhere and it sort of is, but this is something personal to you. The reason behind this is to fully accept what you want as something you will have. The familiarity of seeing your dreams written down all around you makes it more real to your subconscious. What you believe you will get.

It is likely you will encounter thoughts or beliefs that will undermine your successful manifestations. This is very common and just because you recognize a negative thought does not mean all your efforts to manifest are ruined. The first step really is simply noticing these thoughts. By being aware of your thinking you can correct it. I tell people when you find yourself thinking negatively say outloud "delete and uncreate that thought." It sounds silly I know, but it works.

Spend time every day, or multiple times every day if you can, meditating on what you want. Make sure you see things in the present tense, for example don't meditate on "someday I'll have..." but meditate on "I now have..." This is important because it installs that belief in your subconscious mind. If you're always thinking in the future tense you will miss the amazing life you have today. Don't wish your life away, simply make it what you want. If you are new to meditation it might be helpful to find guided meditations to use while you learn the ropes. Years ago I created a "live your perfect life" meditation. It's still on my YouTube channel to this day. Feel free to use that one or find another one you like. The important thing is not which guided meditation you use, it's that you use one.

Finally when you are manifesting you absolutely must have faith that it works. You have to cultivate a belief that everything you are doing will be successful. If you find yourself doubting use the "delete and uncreate" phrase until your doubt is vanquished. Many people have faith in a source or creator being or religion. This is a belief in yourself. It's fine if you are someone who prays or does rituals to go along with your manifesting, but ultimately you must have faith in yourself and what you are creating.

Positive Affirmations

I know I've mentioned positive affirmations several times throughout this book. It just makes sense to include some information about using positive affirmations since we've been talking about energy and raising your vibration.

While you can certainly use positive affirmations for anything I like to have my students begin by using them to raise their vibration. It may seem strange to you to do a positive affirmation to raise your vibration but in all seriousness you are not going to be successful in any manifestions unless your entire being is in alignment and completely believes that you will get what you want. People do like a shortcut after all.

Here's my reasoning. You can do everything correctly in setting up your manifestion. You can journal, work with chakras, get the right crystals, do the right meditations and yet things just don't come together. Why? Well many of us didn't grow up with a great support system. Many of us didn't grow up with people who supported and encouraged our dreams. Often we were probably told we were worthless or stupid or lazy or whatever. All of that gets stored in our subconscious mind.

So years go by and you are all grown up and trying to manifest a better life for yourself. So you do everything you're told to do. But deep inside your subconscious is saying "you can't do that, that will never work, you don't deserve that…" Basically all those negative things you were ever told about yourself. You most likely don't even realize this is happening. So what to do?

First thing that I tell people to do is write down all the negative things anyone ever told you. All of it. Then take a different colored pen (or crayon, make it fun) and put a big "X" through what you've written. Over that write "uncreate and delete." Then know you are at your starting point. Forgive all of those people who were the offenders in your life and let it go. You're done. Congratulations. Repeat as necessary to really feel like you've forgiven and forgotten.

Now you can work with positive affirmations and the first one I want you to work with is:

I AM WORTHY

You have to walk before you can run. Please do yourself a favor and begin at the beginning. If you are like most of the people I work with you've got a lot of negative conditioning to undo. If you're going to train yourself to manifest your dream life you're going to have to believe yourself worthy of doing so. Start here with I am worthy. Write it down, say it out loud, scream it to the heavens. Whatever you have to do to begin to believe you are indeed worthy of whatever you want to be worthy of. There is no time limit so do this as often as you want. Consider it a gift to yourself from yourself.

Another very good affirmation for those who are trying to raise their vibration is:

I LOVE MYSELF

Often when we haven't come from a place that was not exactly kind we begin to believe we are the problem, we start to think we just are not loveable. When you are struggling to believe any of this really works you can probably trace the cause back to a sense of being unloveable. Along with saying I am worthy adding I love myself can help you really get started along this spiritual energetic journey.

If you're one of those life just has not been kind to I recommend using these two affirmations several times every day for at least a week before adding anything others. As I've said before, this is a process and it will likely take some time before things begin to sink in. Please remember this is not a race it is a journey. Don't compare your life to anyone else's and it's probably not a good idea to tell friends and family what you're doing at the beginning either. If they were never supportive in your past they will not be supportive now either and any negative words they might say can derail you completely. If you've come this far in this tiny book you have already dedicated yourself to spiritual growth and raising your vibration. Don't abandon yourself because someone you love can't see the benefit to what you are doing. Changing your programming is already a difficult process for most people, don't make it any more difficult on yourself.

Once you've worked with self-worth and self-love for a while you can move on to other affirmations. You can even make up your own affirmations to use as long as you state them in the present as if what you're working on is already in your life. It's tempting to make affirmations about money, relationships or other things outside of yourself, but in the beginning please resist that temptation. There is plenty of time to create things of this world, trying to focus your energy in that direction in the beginning is likely to be a source of frustration because you are simply not ready yet. It's far more worth it in the long-run to focus on affirmations that heal your soul while you're starting out.

Here are some examples of affirmations that would be appropriate for you at this point:

I am grateful

I deserve success

I am happy

The whole universe is working for me

I trust everything is working out

I am loved

I am supported

I am forgiving

As I mentioned previously you can always make your own affirmations focused on what it is you are manifesting in your life. I have my students and clients work with only one or two affirmations at a time and usually for a week. Don't try to do more than you are ready to do. If you find you are feeling frustrated or angry or agitated you are trying to move too fast. Slow down. This is your life you are working for and it's worth all the time it takes you to make progress. One affirmation I purposely did not include above but that I have given people to work with is "I easily raise my vibration to match what I want to manifest." You can use it if you want, but I've found it's a more complicated affirmation than most beginners can be successful with.   Easiest is best with affirmations, especially in the beginning. I only included it here as an example of what you can do with affirmations.

Final Thoughts

Obviously this has been a very tiny book about a very large and all-encompassing topic. Hopefully you've gleaned at least a few nuggets of knowledge within these pages and it is my sincere hope you continue along this path. It will only make everything in your life better and more fulfilling.

I want to emphasize the importance of setting your intention while doing energy work. It is your intention and your focus on your intention that really makes everything work. You might not know right now exactly what it is that you want. Perhaps you've done a lot in your life and found none of it truly satisfying. That is a lot more common than you think. This is the reason I began with the basics.

Give yourself some time with these basics to really figure yourself out. Allow yourself to play with your imagination and creativity. Become a child again at least for a few minutes each day. Remember what it was like to be hopeful and to have that childlike innocence and belief you could do or be anything. I know there are those of you who didn't have that type of childhood. You weren't allowed to be a child. All the more reason to allow yourself to become a child now for at least a few minutes. Learn to imagine, to play with scenarios for your life. It is the more amazing thing to do for yourself. This will allow you to really discover yourself and what you really do want in life.

Often when people begin this work on themselves they have all sorts of bad memories or repressed trauma surface. This can be very upsetting. Please understand that is all part of healing so you can raise your vibration. So often we bury events from our early lives, sometimes we bury them so deeply we forget all about them. Then we wonder where our lack of self-esteem and self-love come from.

If you are someone who has struggled with self-love and self-esteem know you are not alone, at all. So many of us have deep inner wounds. My belief is that we don't remember them until we are ready to remember. That's why it's usually when we begin a spiritual journey to raise our vibrations all of those things come back into our minds. But again, you have to allow this so you can heal, so you can move forward.

Journaling can help you here. Write down those things can come up for you. Then focus on them, feel them, forgive them and let them go. If you set your intention to do that you will be successful.

Know always that you are loved. If you would like to reach out, I would love to hear from you. My website is www.intuitivemediumkelliefitzgerald.com Good luck on your journey.